W9-BLC-788

5/02

DISCARDED

Rookie
reader

I Can Do It All

Written by Mary E. Pearson
Illustrated by Jeff Shelly

Children's Press®
A Division of Scholastic Inc.
New York • Toronto • London • Auckland • Sydney
Mexico City • New Delhi • Hong Kong
Danbury, Connecticut

To every librarian who has led a child into a world
of books and said, "Dream . . . believe."
— M.E.P.

To Christine
— J.S.

Reading Consultants

Linda Cornwell
Literacy Specialist

Katharine A. Kane
Education Consultant
(Retired, San Diego County Office of Education and San Diego State University)

Library of Congress Cataloging-in-Publication Data
Pearson, Mary (Mary E.)
    I can do it all / written by Mary E. Pearson ; illustrated by Jeff Shelly.
        p. cm. — (Rookie reader)
    Summary: When a boy goes to the library, he realizes he can pretend to be and to do
anything by reading books.
    ISBN 0-516-22240-6 (lib. bdg.)   0-516-27383-3 (pbk.)
    [1. Libraries—Fiction. 2. Books and reading—Fiction. 3. Stories in rhyme.]
I. Shelly, Jeff, ill. II. Title. III. Series.
PZ8.3.P27472 lae 2001
[E]—dc21   2001003836

© 2002 by Children's Press®, a division of Scholastic Inc.
Illustrations © 2002 by Jeff Shelly
All rights reserved. Published simultaneously in Canada.
Printed in the United States of America.
1 2 3 4 5 6 7 8 9 10 R 11 10 09 08 07 06 05 04 03 02

I zoom in a plane.

3

I sail on a ship.

I race a fast car.

I take a space trip.

9

I hike in the desert.

I dive in the sea.

12

13

I swing in a jungle.

14

I climb a tall tree.

I pan with a miner.

19

I dance in a show.

20

I hold a big boa.

I make the best throw!

I guard an old castle.

28

I visit the king.

When I go to the library,
I can do anything!

31

Word List (50 words)

a	do	old	throw
all	fast	on	to
an	go	pan	tree
anything	guard	plane	trip
best	hike	race	visit
big	hold	sail	when
boa	I	sea	with
can	in	ship	zoom
car	it	show	
castle	jungle	space	
climb	king	swing	
dance	library	take	
desert	make	tall	
dive	miner	the	

About the Author

Mary E. Pearson is a writer and teacher in San Diego, California.

About the Illustrator

Jeff Shelly was born in Lancaster, Pennsylvania, and grew up looking at the humorous side of life. He worked as an animator for many years and now works as an illustrator. Jeff lives with his wife, Christine, and his two dachshunds, Jessie and James, in Hollywood, California.